ANiMAL ANATOMY

ANIMAL ANATOMY

SNIFF TIPS, RUNNING STICKS, AND OTHER ACCURATELY NAMED ANIMAL PARTS

SOPHIE CORRIGAN

CHRONICLE BOOKS

SAN FRANCISCO

ANATOMY OF AN
ATOM

SPECIAL
SINGLE-CELLED
WONDER

ANATOMY OF ye OLDe
FiSHY-KiNS

TiNY BASiC SWiMMY WiggLeR
FiLLeD WiTH POTeNTIAL

ANATOMY OF ye OLDe
PRiMORDiAL SQUiSHeR

PRiMiTive
Leg SegMeNTS

SWiMMY STePPeRS

LiTTLe Jiggly

ANATOMY OF A
MUDSKIPPER

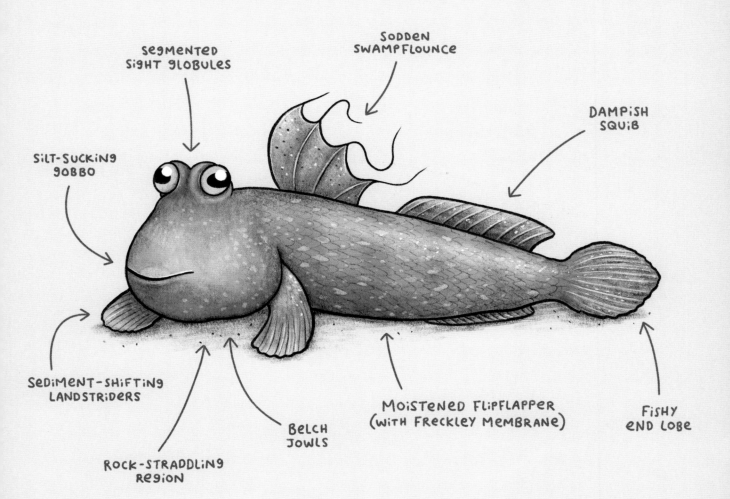

Segmented Sight Globules

Sodden Swampflounce

Dampish Squib

Silt-Sucking Gobbo

Sediment-Shifting Landstriders

Rock-Straddling Region

Belch Jowls

Moistened Flipflapper (with Freckley Membrane)

Fishy End Lobe

ANATOMY OF ye OLDE
AMPHiBiOUS BLOB

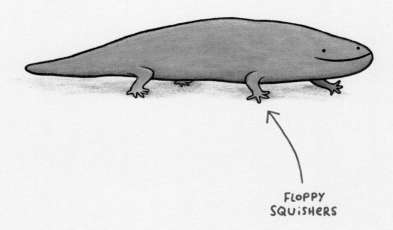

FLOPPY
SQUiSHERS

ANATOMY OF ye OLDe
RePTILLiAN SCUTTLeR

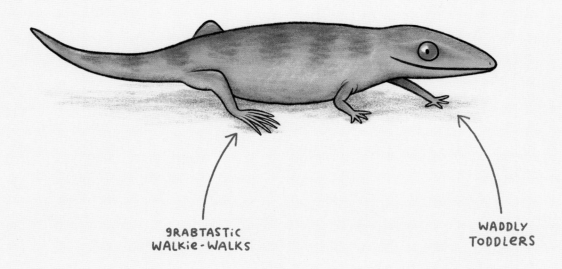

9RABTASTiC
WALKie-WALKS

WADDLY
TODDLeRS

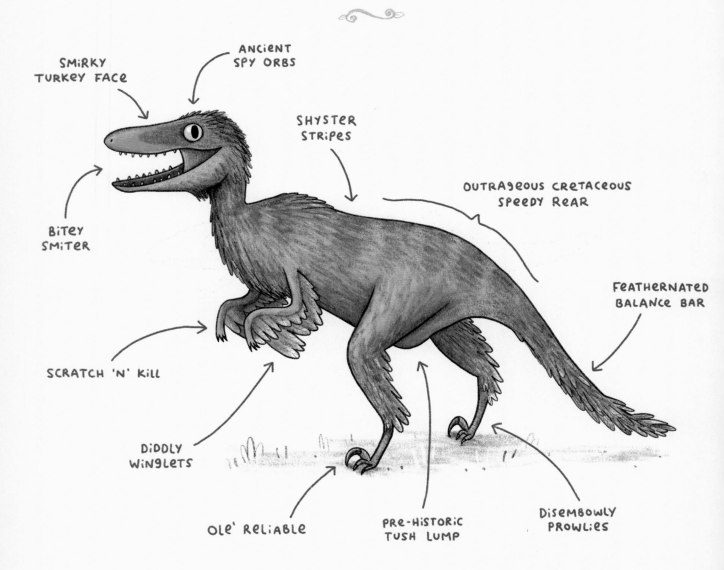

ANATOMY OF A
VELOCiRAPTOR

SMiRKY
TURKEY FACE

ANCiENT
SPY ORBS

SHYSTER
STRiPeS

OUTRAGeOUS CReTACeOUS
SPeeDY ReAR

BiTeY
SMiTeR

FeATHeRNATeD
BALANCe BAR

SCRATCH 'N' KiLL

DiDDLY
WiNGLeTS

OLe' ReLiABLe

PRe-HiSTORiC
TUSH LUMP

DiSeMBOWLY
PROWLieS

ANATOMY OF A
TYRANNOSAURUS REX

(AKA GODZILLA'S OLDER BROTHER)

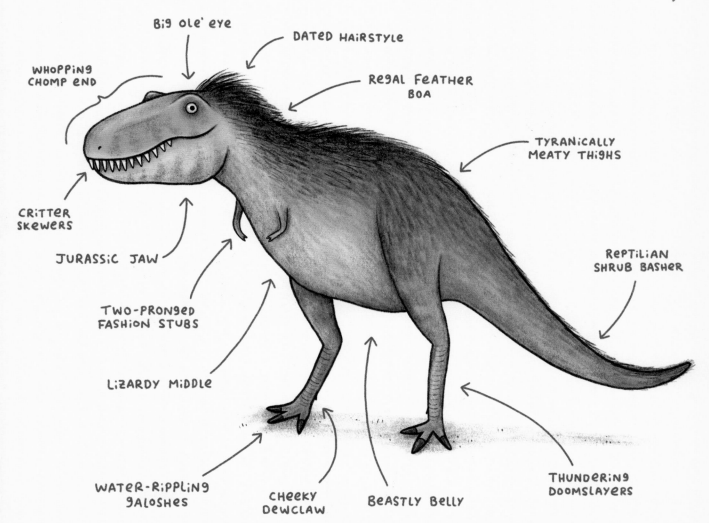

Big ole' eye

DATED HAIRSTYLE

WHOPPING CHOMP END

REGAL FEATHER BOA

TYRANICALLY MEATY THIGHS

CRITTER SKEWERS

JURASSIC JAW

REPTILIAN SHRUB BASHER

TWO-PRONGED FASHION STUBS

LIZARDY MIDDLE

WATER-RIPPLING GALOSHES

CHEEKY DEWCLAW

BEASTLY BELLY

THUNDERING DOOMSLAYERS

ANATOMY OF A
CHICKEN

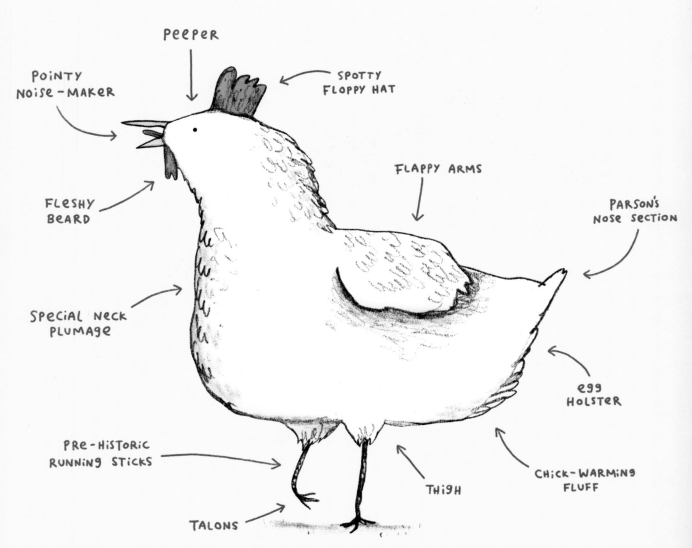

PEEPER

POINTY
NOISE-MAKER

SPOTTY
FLOPPY HAT

FLESHY
BEARD

FLAPPY ARMS

PARSON'S
NOSE SECTION

SPECIAL NECK
PLUMAGE

egg
HOLSTER

PRE-HISTORIC
RUNNING STICKS

THIGH

CHICK-WARMING
FLUFF

TALONS

FIND A CHICKEN,
PICK IT UP...

AND ALL THE DAY
YOU'LL HAVE GOOD CLUCK.

ANATOMY OF A

COW

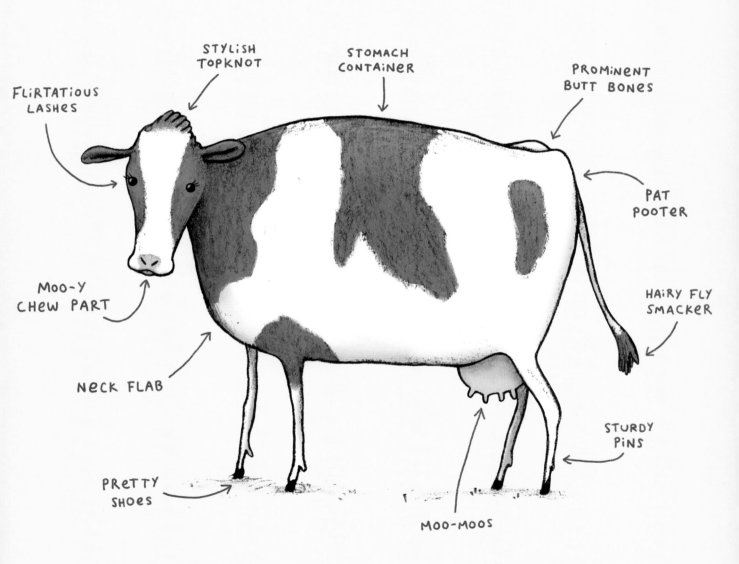

ANATOMY OF A
HORSE

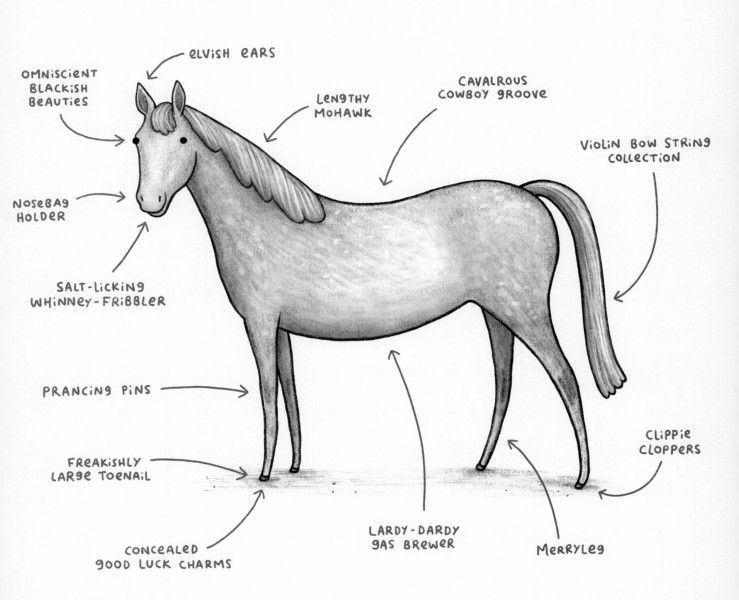

ELVISH EARS

OMNISCIENT
BLACKISH
BEAUTIES

LENGTHY
MOHAWK

CAVALROUS
COWBOY GROOVE

VIOLIN BOW STRING
COLLECTION

NOSEBAG
HOLDER

SALT-LICKING
WHINNEY-FRIBBLER

PRANCING PINS

FREAKISHLY
LARGE TOENAIL

CLIPPIE
CLOPPERS

CONCEALED
GOOD LUCK CHARMS

LARDY-DARDY
GAS BREWER

MERRYLEG

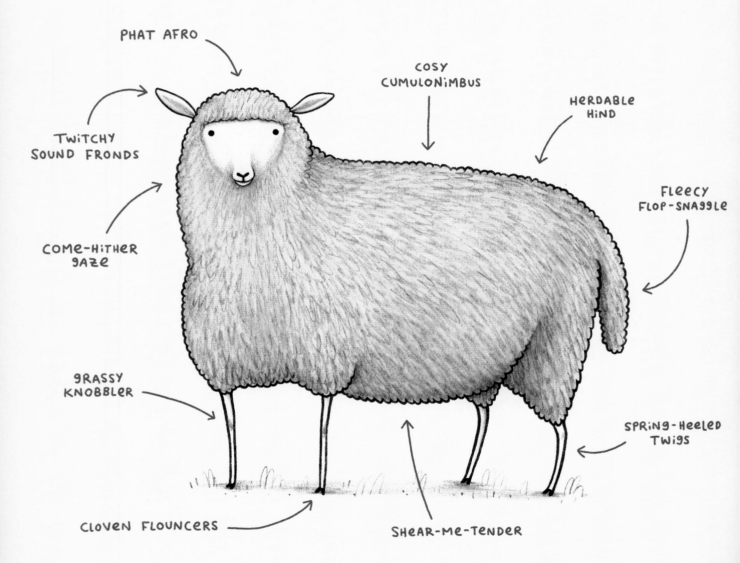

RAMUEL

ewenice

LAMBUEL

THE SHEEPS

ALWAYS BEWARE
A WOLF iN SHEEP'S CLOTHiNG,
AND ViCE VERSA.

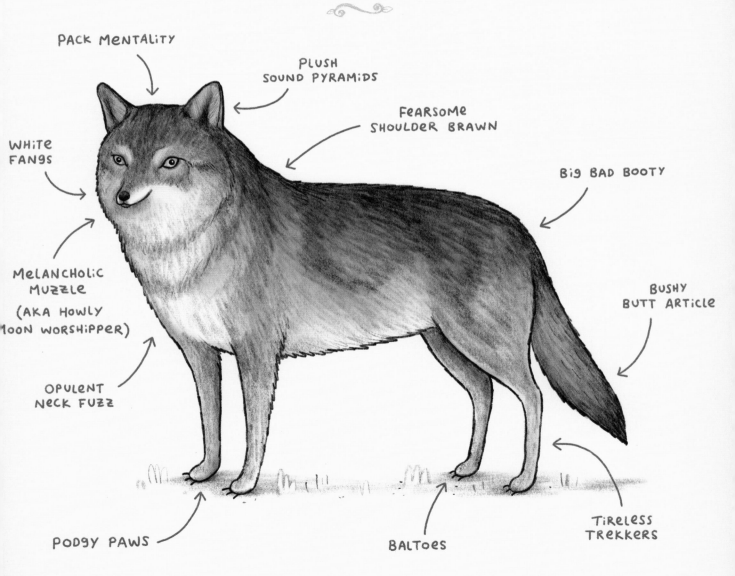

ANATOMY OF A
WOLF

PACK MENTALITY

PLUSH
SOUND PYRAMIDS

FEARSOME
SHOULDER BRAWN

BIG BAD BOOTY

WHITE
FANGS

MELANCHOLIC
MUZZLE
(AKA HOWLY
MOON WORSHIPPER)

BUSHY
BUTT ARTICLE

OPULENT
NECK FUZZ

PODGY PAWS

BALTOES

TIRELESS
TREKKERS

ANATOMY OF A
Pig

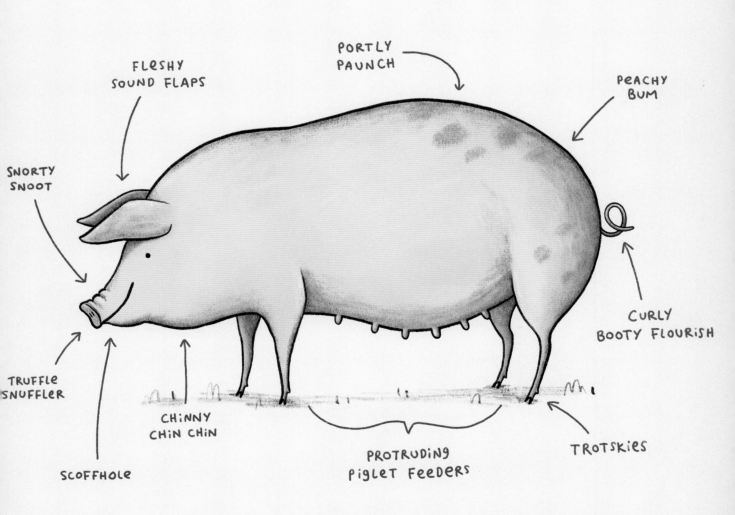

FLESHY
SOUND FLAPS

PORTLY
PAUNCH

PEACHY
BUM

SNORTY
SNOOT

TRUFFLE
SNUFFLER

SCOFFHOLE

CHINNY
CHIN CHIN

PROTRUDING
PIGLET FEEDERS

TROTSKIES

CURLY
BOOTY FLOURISH

ANATOMY OF A
WEASEL

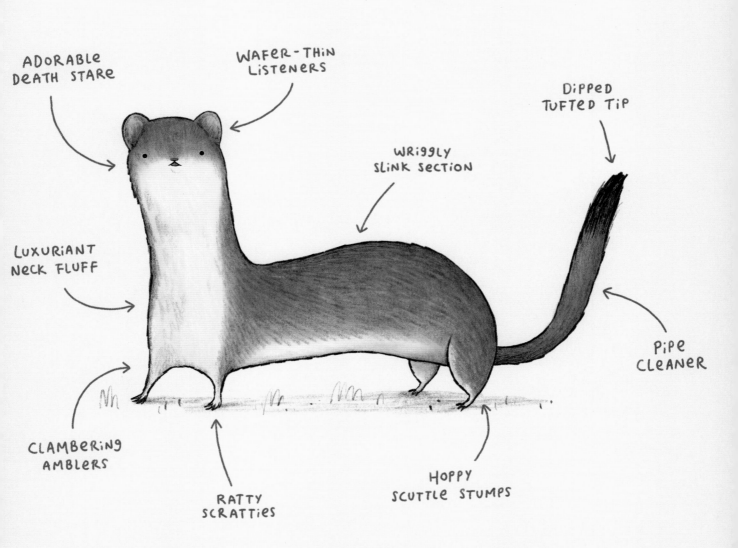

ADORABLE
DEATH STARE

WAFER-THIN
LISTENERS

DIPPED
TUFTED TIP

WRIGGLY
SLINK SECTION

LUXURIANT
NECK FLUFF

PIPE
CLEANER

CLAMBERING
AMBLERS

RATTY
SCRATTIES

HOPPY
SCUTTLE STUMPS

ANATOMY OF A RABBIT

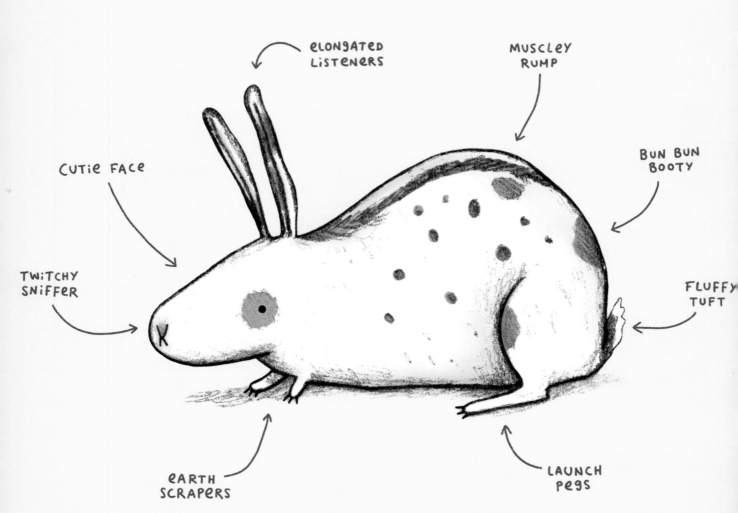

elongated
listeners

muscley
rump

cutie face

BUN BUN
BOOTY

twitchy
sniffer

FLUFFY
TUFT

earth
scrapers

LAUNCH
pegs

ANATOMY OF A
FOX

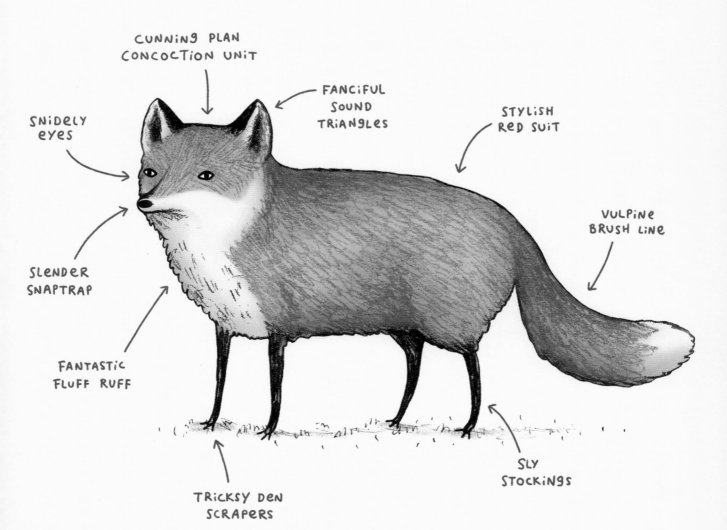

CUNNING PLAN
CONCOCTION UNIT

FANCIFUL
SOUND
TRIANGLES

STYLISH
RED SUIT

SNIDELY
EYES

VULPINE
BRUSH LINE

SLENDER
SNAPTRAP

FANTASTIC
FLUFF RUFF

TRICKSY DEN
SCRAPERS

SLY
STOCKINGS

THERE'S NO SUCH THING
AS AN 'UGLY DUCKLING.'

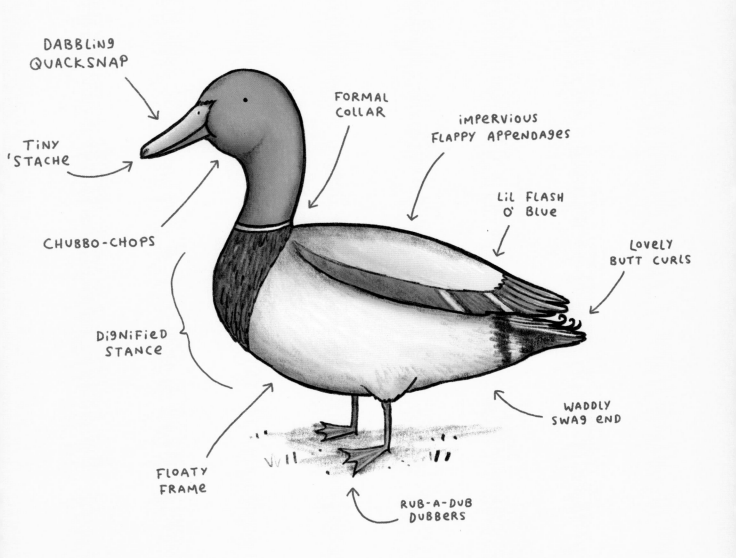

ANATOMY OF A
FiELD MOUSE

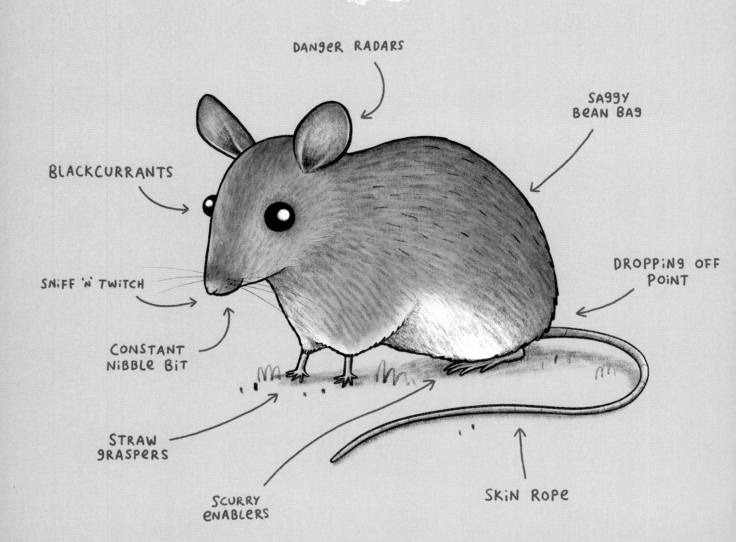

DANGER RADARS

SAGGY BEAN BAG

BLACKCURRANTS

SNIFF 'N' TWITCH

CONSTANT NIBBLE BIT

DROPPING OFF POINT

STRAW GRASPERS

SCURRY ENABLERS

SKIN ROPE

ANATOMY OF A
guinea pig

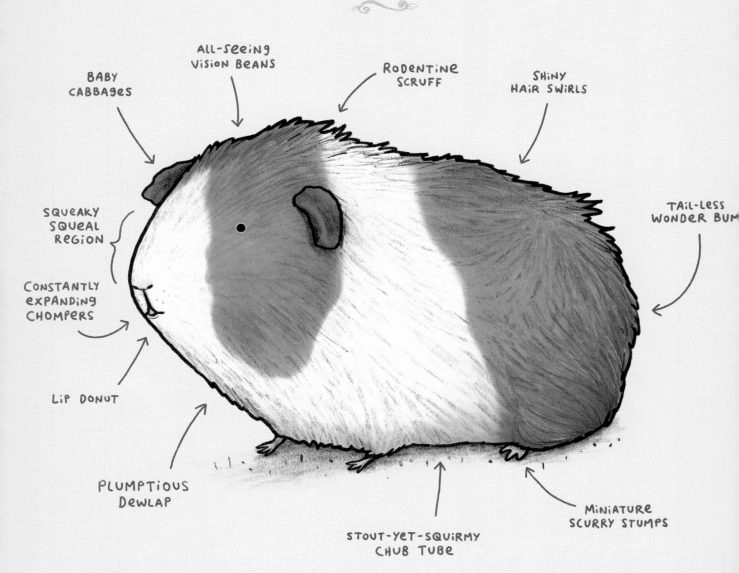

BABY CABBAGES

ALL-SEEING VISION BEANS

RODENTINE SCRUFF

SHINY HAIR SWIRLS

SQUEAKY SQUEAL REGION

CONSTANTLY EXPANDING CHOMPERS

TAIL-LESS WONDER BUM

LIP DONUT

PLUMPTIOUS DEWLAP

STOUT-YET-SQUIRMY CHUB TUBE

MINIATURE SCURRY STUMPS

ANATOMY OF A
GOAT

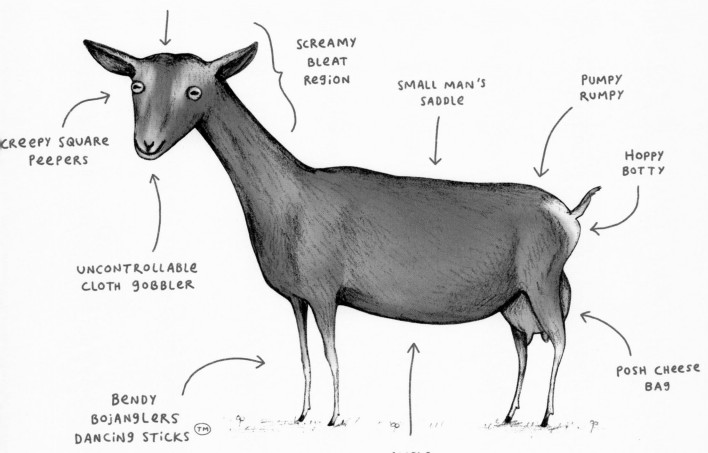

VIOLENT BASHCAP

SCREAMY BLEAT REGION

SMALL MAN'S SADDLE

PUMPY RUMPY

HOPPY BOTTY

CREEPY SQUARE PEEPERS

UNCONTROLLABLE CLOTH GOBBLER

BENDY BOJANGLERS DANCING STICKS ™

AMPLE COLLYWOBBLER

POSH CHEESE BAG

ANATOMY OF A
LLAMA

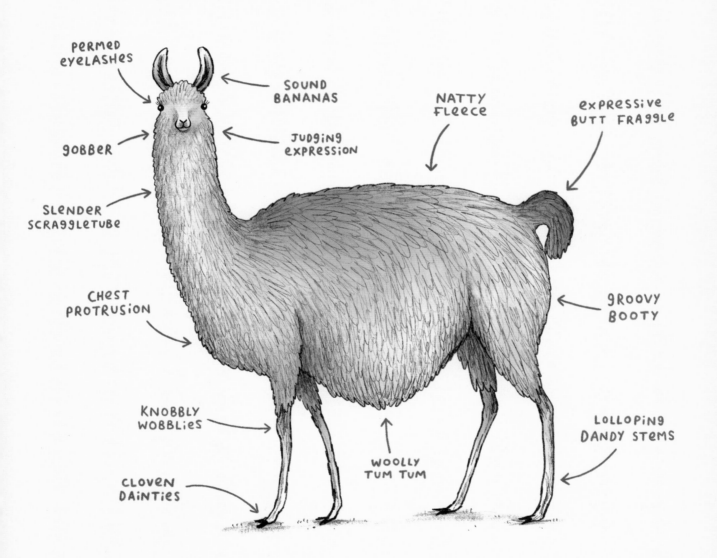

PERMED EYELASHES

SOUND BANANAS

NATTY FLEECE

EXPRESSIVE BUTT FRAGGLE

GOBBER

JUDGING EXPRESSION

SLENDER SCRAGGLETUBE

CHEST PROTRUSION

GROOVY BOOTY

KNOBBLY WOBBLIES

WOOLLY TUM TUM

LOLLOPING DANDY STEMS

CLOVEN DAINTIES

ANATOMY OF AN
EARTHWORM

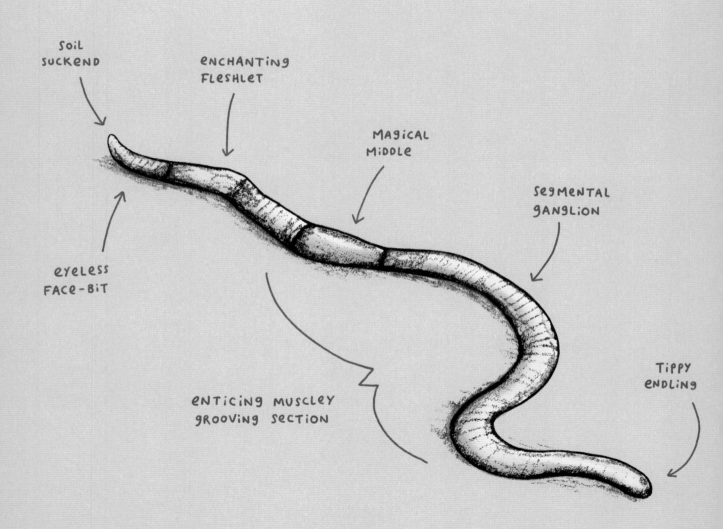

Soil
suckend

enchanting
fleshlet

Magical
Middle

segmental
ganglion

eyeless
Face-Bit

enticing muscley
grooving section

Tippy
endling

ANATOMY OF A
MOLE

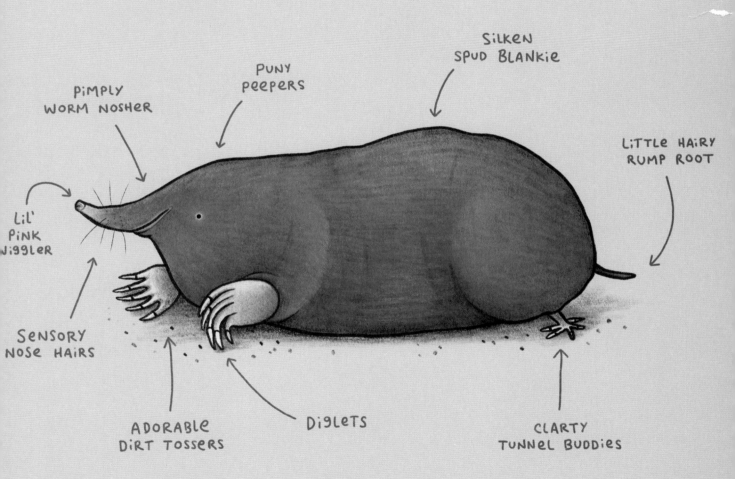

SILKEN
SPUD BLANKIE

PUNY
PEEPERS

PIMPLY
WORM NOSHER

LITTLE HAIRY
RUMP ROOT

Lil'
PINK
WIGGLER

SENSORY
NOSE HAIRS

ADORABLE
DIRT TOSSERS

DIGLETS

CLARTY
TUNNEL BUDDIES

ANATOMY OF A
VAMPIRE BAT

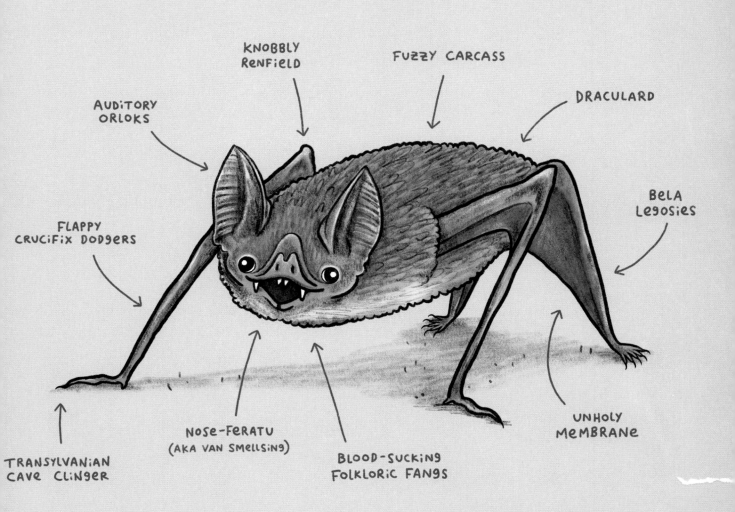

KNOBBLY
ReNFieLD

FUZZY CARCASS

DRACULARD

AUDiTORY
ORLOKS

BeLA
LegoSieS

FLAPPY
CRUCiFix DoDgeRS

Nose-FeRATU
(AKA VAN SMeLLSiNg)

BLOOD-SUCKiNg
FOLKLORiC FANgS

UNHOLY
MeMBRANe

TRANSYLVANiAN
CAVe CLiNgeR

ANATOMY OF A
HEDGEHOG

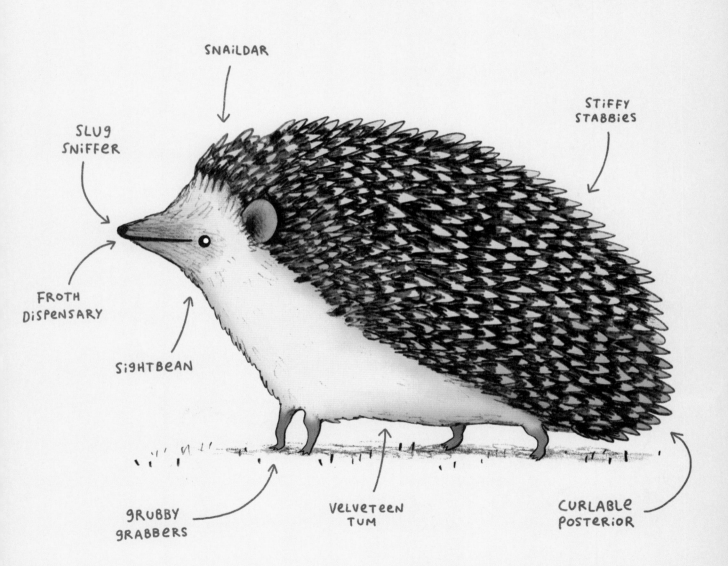

SNAILDAR

STIFFY
STABBIES

SLUG
SNIFFER

FROTH
DISPENSARY

SIGHTBEAN

GRUBBY
GRABBERS

VELVETEEN
TUM

CURLABLE
POSTERIOR

ANATOMY OF A
PUg

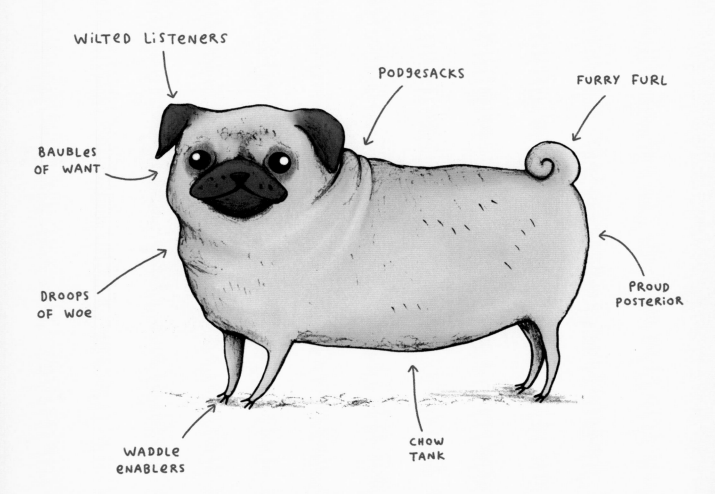

WILTED LISTENERS

PODGESACKS

FURRY FURL

BAUBLES
OF WANT

DROOPS
OF WOE

PROUD
POSTERIOR

WADDLE
ENABLERS

CHOW
TANK

ANATOMY OF A
DACHSHUND

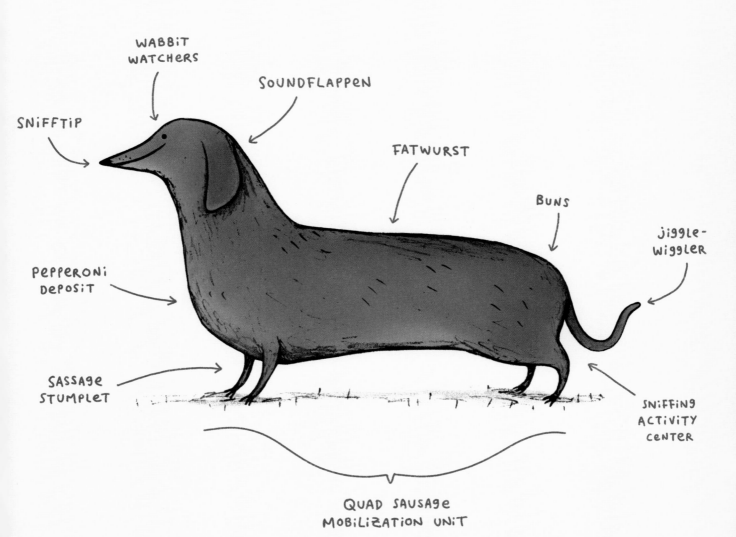

WABBIT
WATCHERS

SOUNDFLAPPEN

SNIFFTIP

FATWURST

BUNS

Jiggle-
Wiggler

PEPPERONI
DEPOSIT

SASSAGE
STUMPLET

SNIFFING
ACTIVITY
CENTER

QUAD SAUSAGE
MOBILIZATION UNIT

ANATOMY OF A
COCKATIEL

VIGILANT MEAL SPOTTERS

NYMPHICAL QUIVERING EXPRESSION WHISP

SHY BLUSHING TICKLEBIT

FRENZIED FLAPSTATION

NIBBLY SQUEAKER

EMBARASSING POOP CONCEALER

DELICATE WAGGLY END

PUFFY FOOD-BULGE

FLUFFY PANTS

HOOK-ENDED GRASPLINGS

ANATOMY OF A
KANGAROO

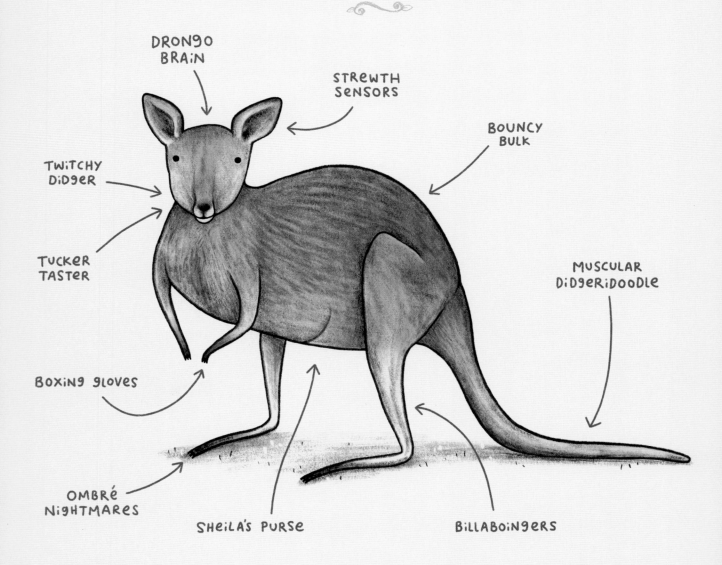

DRONGO BRAIN

STREWTH SENSORS

BOUNCY BULK

TWITCHY DIDGER

TUCKER TASTER

MUSCULAR DIDGERIDOODLE

BOXING GLOVES

OMBRÉ NIGHTMARES

SHEILA'S PURSE

BILLABOINGERS

ANATOMY OF A
TREE FROG

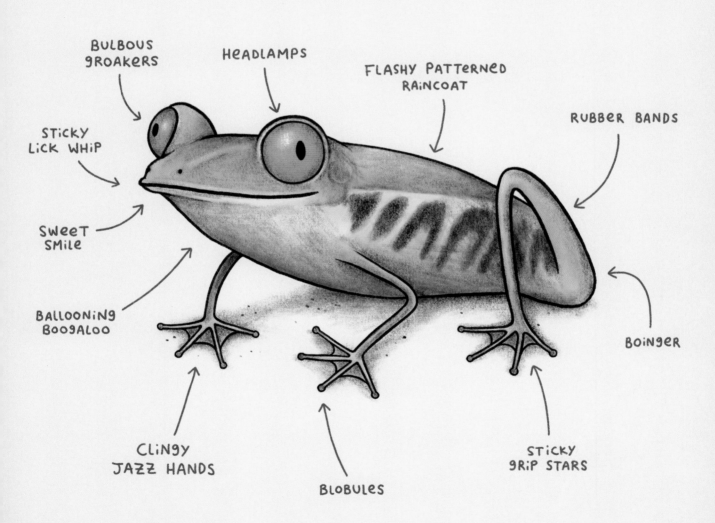

BULBOUS
GROAKERS

HEADLAMPS

FLASHY PATTERNED
RAINCOAT

RUBBER BANDS

STICKY
LICK WHIP

SWEET
SMILE

BALLOONING
BOOGALOO

CLINGY
JAZZ HANDS

BLOBULES

STICKY
GRIP STARS

BOINGER

ANATOMY OF A
KiWi BiRD

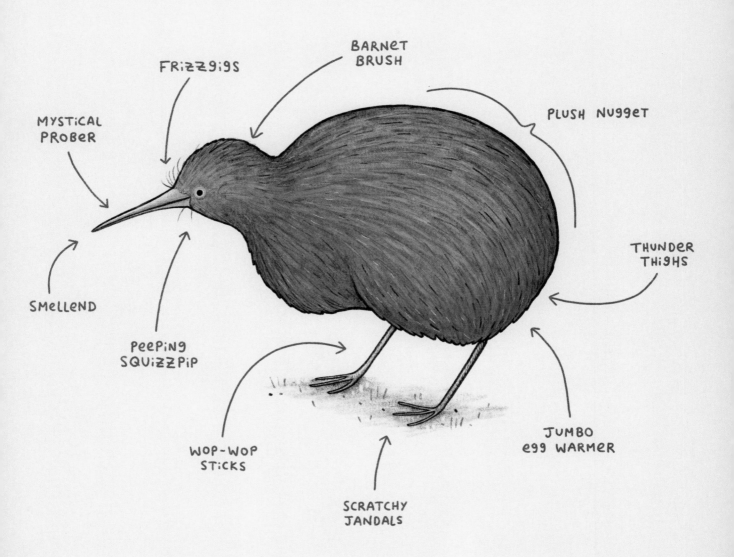

OCELITTLE

OCELOT

ANATOMY OF A
CROCODILE

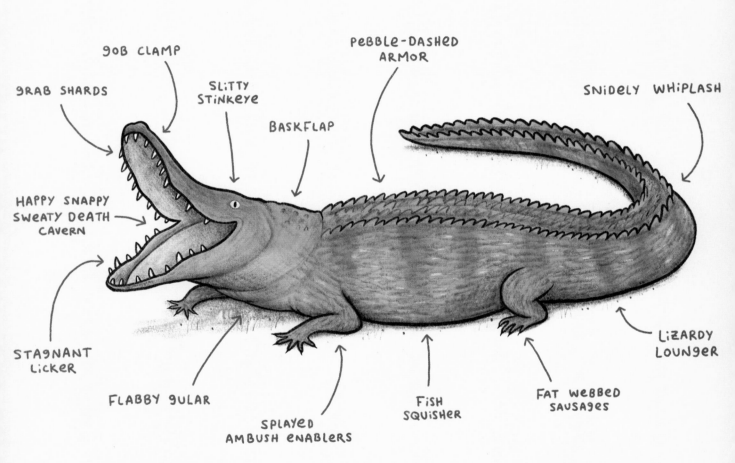

GOB CLAMP

GRAB SHARDS

SLITTY STINKEYE

PEBBLE-DASHED ARMOR

BASKFLAP

SNIDELY WHIPLASH

HAPPY SNAPPY SWEATY DEATH CAVERN

STAGNANT LICKER

FLABBY GULAR

SPLAYED AMBUSH ENABLERS

FISH SQUISHER

FAT WEBBED SAUSAGES

LIZARDY LOUNGER

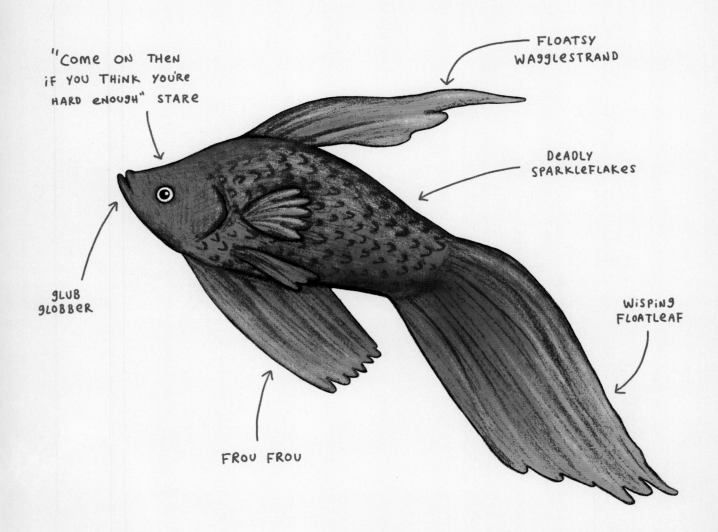

ANATOMY OF A
BETTA FISH

FLOATSY
WAGGLESTRAND

"COME ON THEN
iF YOU THiNK YOU'RE
HARD ENOUGH" STARE

DEADLY
SPARKLEFLAKES

GLUB
GLOBBER

WiSPiNG
FLOATLEAF

FROU FROU

ANATOMY OF A
LOBSTER

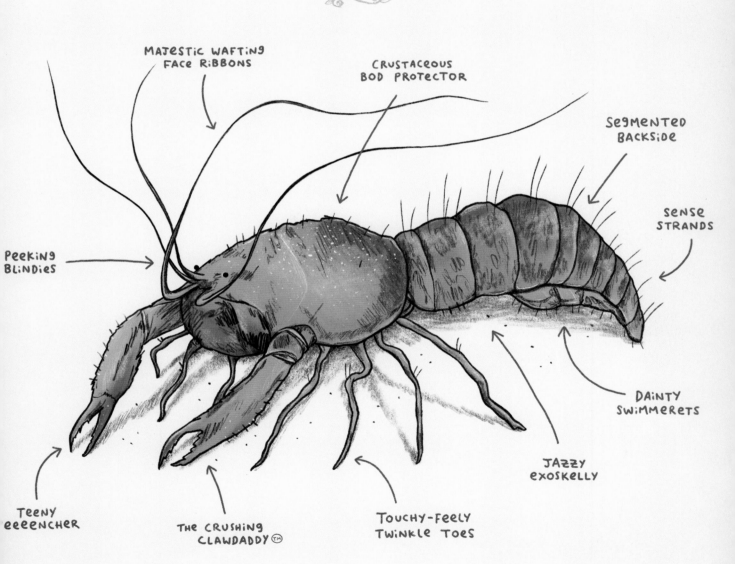

MAJESTIC WAFTING FACE RIBBONS

CRUSTACEOUS BOD PROTECTOR

SEGMENTED BACKSIDE

SENSE STRANDS

PEEKING BLINDIES

DAINTY SWIMMERETS

JAZZY EXOSKELLY

TEENY EEEENCHER

THE CRUSHING CLAWDADDY ™

TOUCHY-FEELY TWINKLE TOES

ANATOMY OF A
SLOTH

THERE'S A SPECIAL KIND OF MOTH
THAT LIVES SOLELY UPON A SLOTH.

IT IS CREATIVELY NAMED THE 'SLOTH MOTH.'

SLOTHS ARE EQUALLY CUTE AND CREEPY.

ANATOMY OF A
LiON

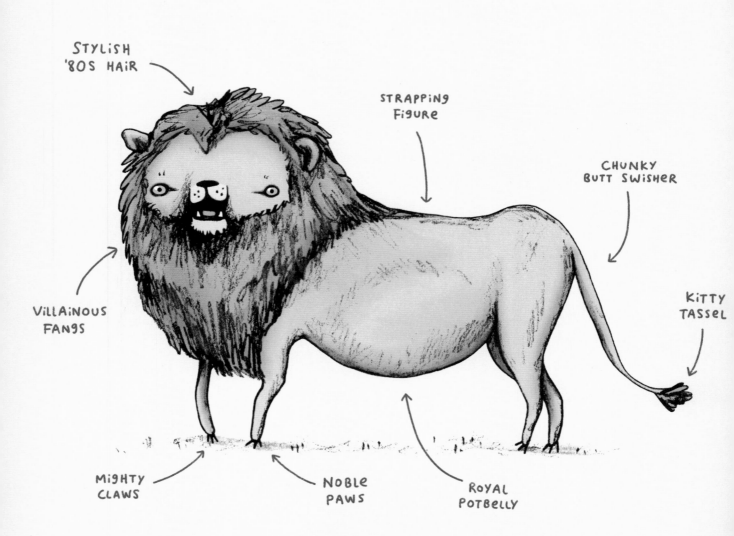

STYLiSH
'80S HAiR

STRAPPiNG
FiGURE

CHUNKY
BUTT SWiSHER

ViLLAiNOUS
FANGS

KiTTY
TASSEL

MiGHTY
CLAWS

NOBLE
PAWS

ROYAL
POTBELLY

ANATOMY OF A GIRAFFE

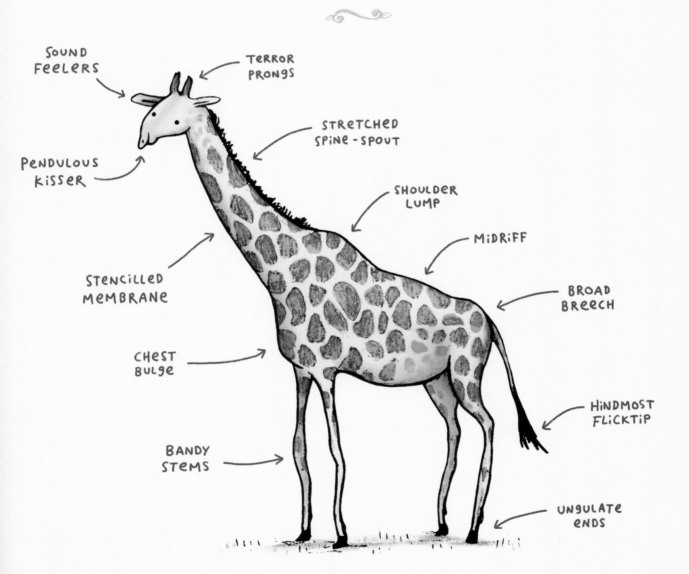

SOUND FEELERS

TERROR PRONGS

STRETCHED SPINE-SPOUT

PENDULOUS KISSER

SHOULDER LUMP

MIDRIFF

STENCILLED MEMBRANE

BROAD BREECH

CHEST BULGE

HINDMOST FLICKTIP

BANDY STEMS

UNGULATE ENDS

HYENA

LOWENA

BABY ELEPHANTS SUCK THEIR FACE NOODLES FOR COMFORT,
LIKE A BABY HUMAN SUCKS THEIR THUMB.

ANATOMY OF AN
eLePHANT

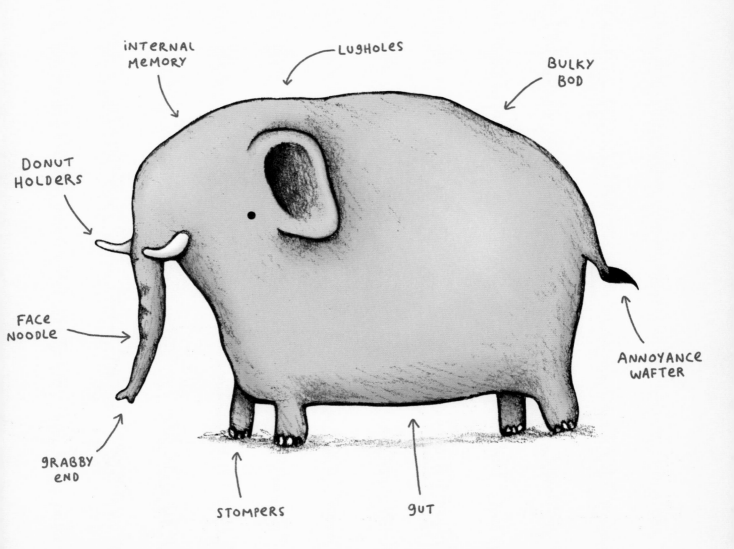

INTERNAL MEMORY

LUGHOLES

BULKY BOD

DONUT HOLDERS

FACE NOODLE

ANNOYANCE WAFTER

GRABBY END

STOMPERS

GUT

THe ADORABLE RUMORS ARE TRUE.

eLePHANTS DO THiS:

AS THEY ARE ACTUALLY MEGA TEETH,
AN ELEPHANT'S DONUT HOLDERS SHOULD <u>NEVER</u>
BE USED TO ACTUALLY HOLD DONUTS,
OR ANYTHING WITH A HIGH SUGAR CONTENT,
AS THIS CAN CAUSE JUMBO TOOTHACHE.

ANATOMY OF A
RHiNOCeROS

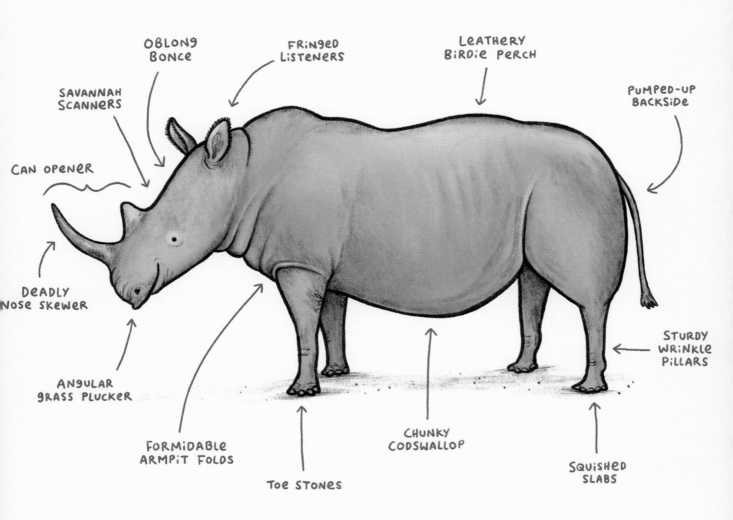

OBLONG
BONCE

FRINGED
LISTENERS

LEATHERY
BIRDIE PERCH

SAVANNAH
SCANNERS

PUMPED-UP
BACKSIDE

CAN OPENER

DEADLY
NOSE SKEWER

ANGULAR
GRASS PLUCKER

FORMIDABLE
ARMPIT FOLDS

TOE STONES

CHUNKY
CODSWALLOP

STURDY
WRINKLE
PILLARS

SQUISHED
SLABS

HUGAPOTAMUS?

SEAHORSES TRAVEL HOLDING ONTO
THEIR OTHER HALF'S GRIP CURL.

ANATOMY OF A
SEAHORSE

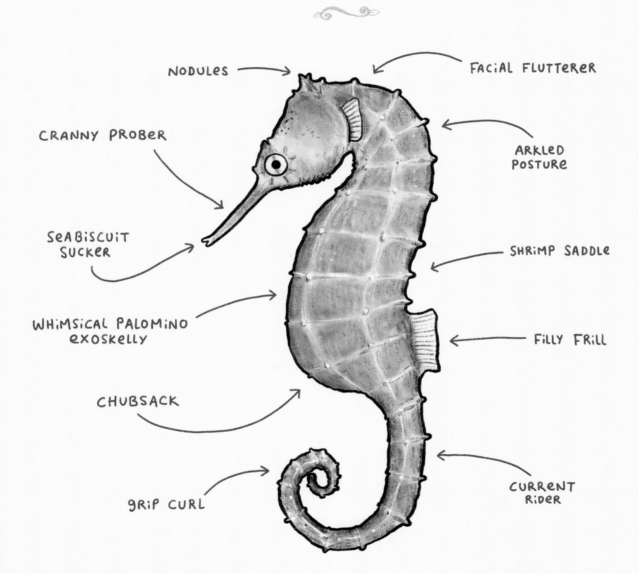

NODULES

FACIAL FLUTTERER

CRANNY PROBER

ARKLED POSTURE

SEABISCUIT SUCKER

SHRIMP SADDLE

WHIMSICAL PALOMINO exoskelly

FILLY FRILL

CHUBSACK

CURRENT RIDER

GRIP CURL

ANATOMY OF A

WALRUS

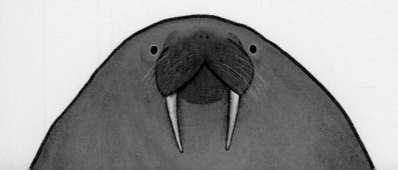

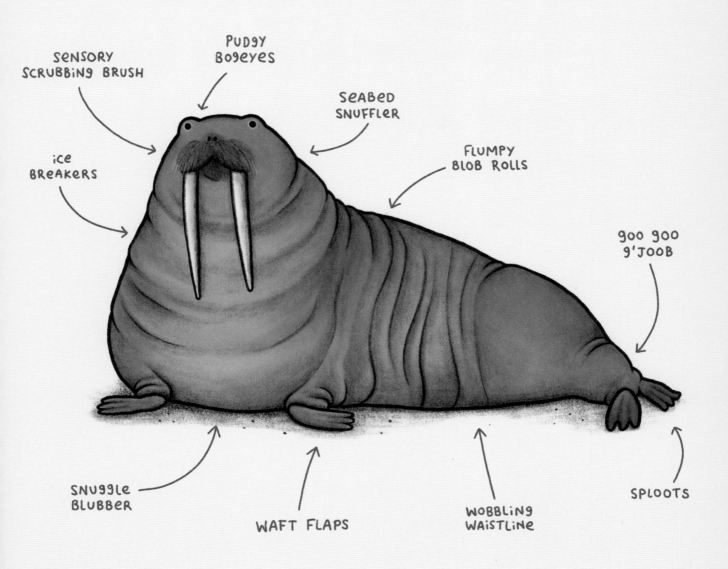

ANATOMY OF A
BELUGA WHALE

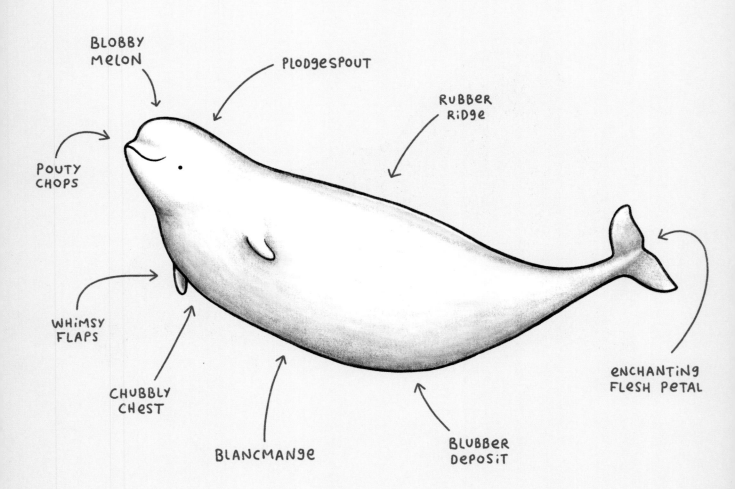

BLOBBY MELON

PLODGESPOUT

RUBBER RIDGE

POUTY CHOPS

WHIMSY FLAPS

CHUBBLY CHEST

BLANCMANGE

BLUBBER DEPOSIT

ENCHANTING FLESH PETAL

ANATOMY OF A
NARWHAL

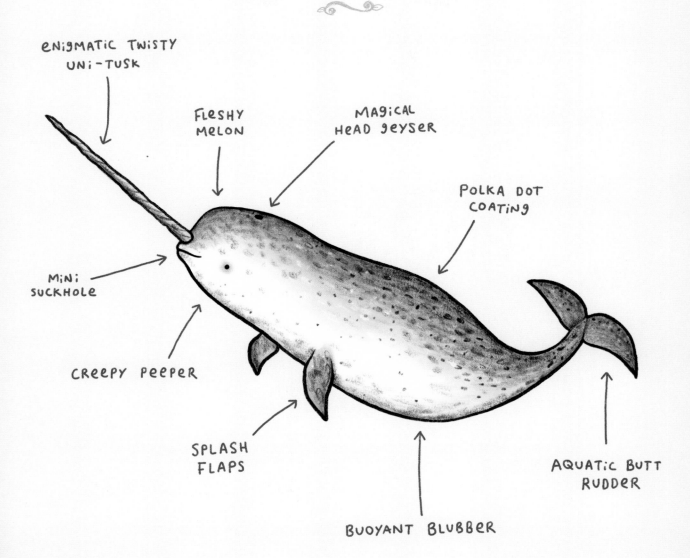

enigmatic twisty
uni-tusk

Fleshy
Melon

Magical
Head Geyser

Polka Dot
Coating

Mini
Suckhole

Creepy Peeper

Splash
Flaps

Buoyant Blubber

Aquatic Butt
Rudder

ANATOMY OF A
POLAR BEAR

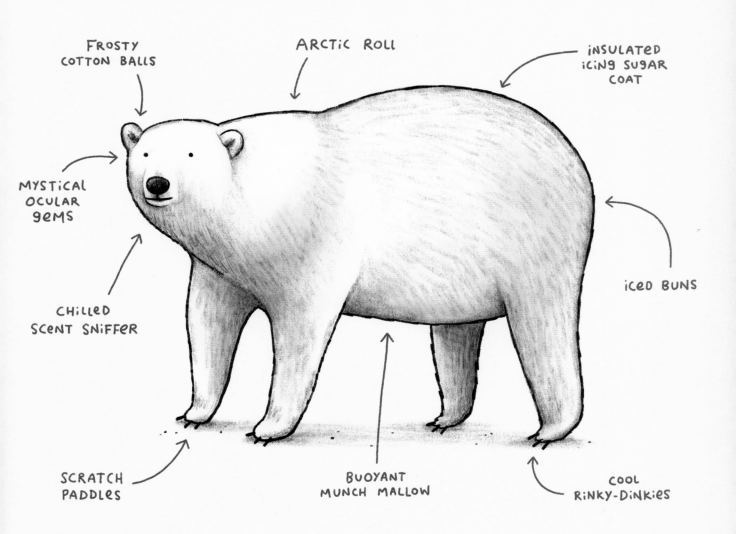

FROSTY
COTTON BALLS

ARCTIC ROLL

INSULATED
ICING SUGAR
COAT

MYSTICAL
OCULAR
GEMS

CHILLED
SCENT SNIFFER

ICED BUNS

SCRATCH
PADDLES

BUOYANT
MUNCH MALLOW

COOL
RINKY-DINKIES

ANATOMY OF A
King Penguin

STRIPED
FISH FINDER
(AKA NOOT NOOT)

POLAR
PEEPERS

ART DECO
AESTHETIC

POINTED
PEBBLE PICK-END

TURBO
FLIPPERFLAP

iced
HUDDLE CRAVER

SCRAGGLE
WEDGE

WADDLE CHUNKS
(WITH CHARLIE CHAPLIN
WALK ACTION)

RUBBERY
GODZILLA TOES

ANATOMY OF A
KiNg VULTURe

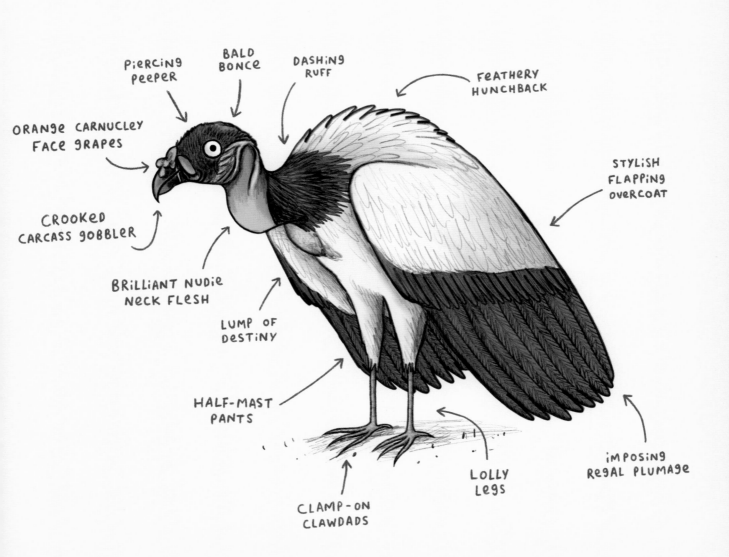

PieRCiNg PeePeR

BALD BONCe

DASHiNg RUFF

FEATHeRY HUNCHBACK

ORANge CARNUCLeY FACe gRAPes

STYLiSH FLAPPiNg OveRCOAT

CROOKeD CARCASS gOBBLeR

BRiLLiANT NUDie NeCK FLeSH

LUMP OF DeSTiNY

HALF-MAST PANTS

CLAMP-ON CLAWDADS

LOLLY LegS

iMPOSiNg RegAL PLUMAge

ANATOMY OF AN
AXOLOTL

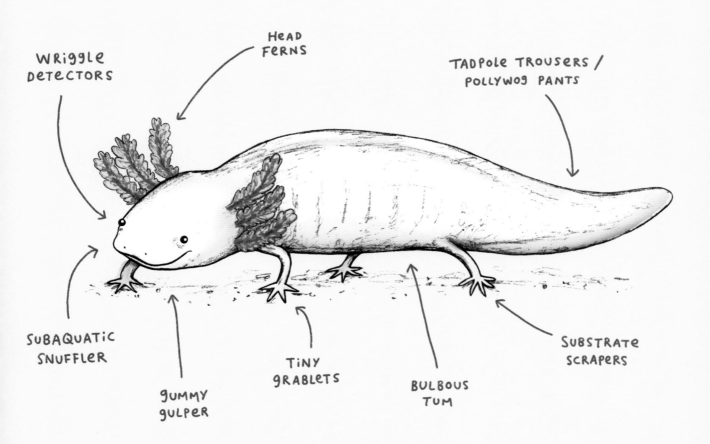

WRIGGLE
DETECTORS

HEAD
FERNS

TADPOLE TROUSERS /
POLLYWOG PANTS

SUBAQUATIC
SNUFFLER

GUMMY
GULPER

TINY
GRABLETS

BULBOUS
TUM

SUBSTRATE
SCRAPERS

AXOLiTTLe

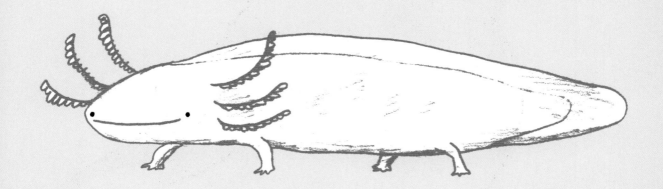

AXOLOTL

ANATOMY OF A
ROBIN

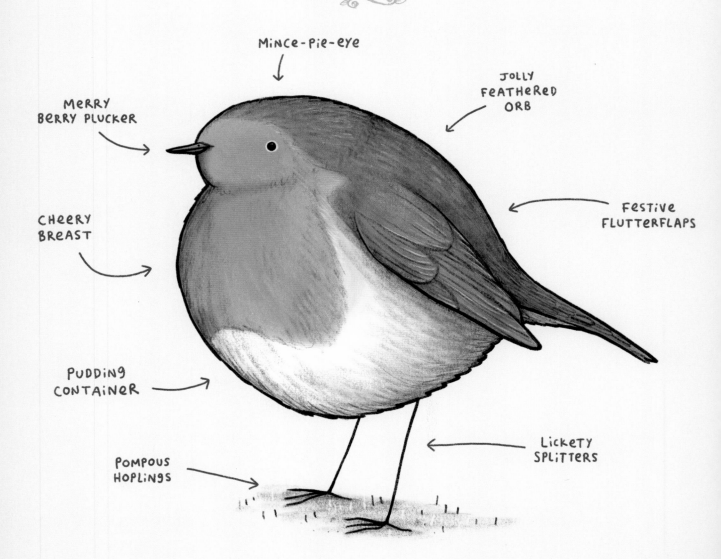

Mince-pie-eye

Merry Berry Plucker

Cheery Breast

Pudding Container

Pompous Hoplings

Jolly Feathered Orb

Festive Flutterflaps

Lickety Splitters

ANATOMY OF AN
OSTRiCH

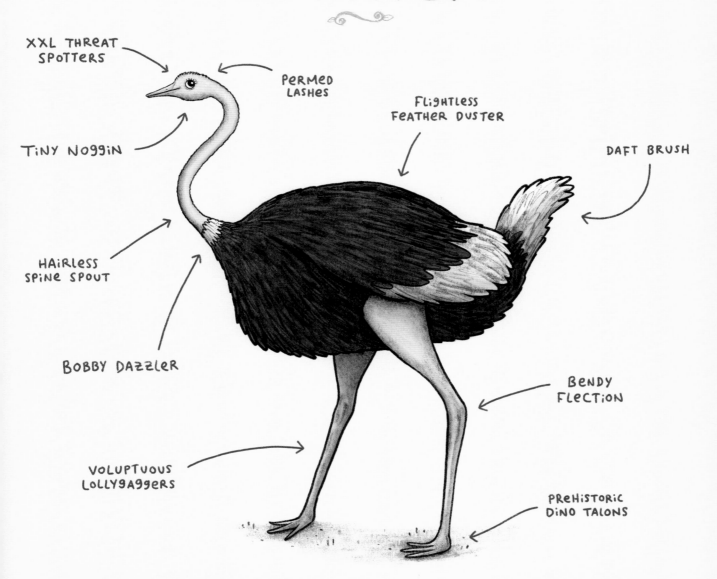

XXL THREAT SPOTTERS

PERMED LASHES

FLIGHTLESS FEATHER DUSTER

DAFT BRUSH

TINY NOGGIN

HAIRLESS SPINE SPOUT

BOBBY DAZZLER

BENDY FLECTION

VOLUPTUOUS LOLLYGAGGERS

PREHISTORIC DINO TALONS

ANATOMY OF A

WOMBAT

FUN FACT: WOMBATS DO DEAR LITTLE CUBE-SHAPED POOPS

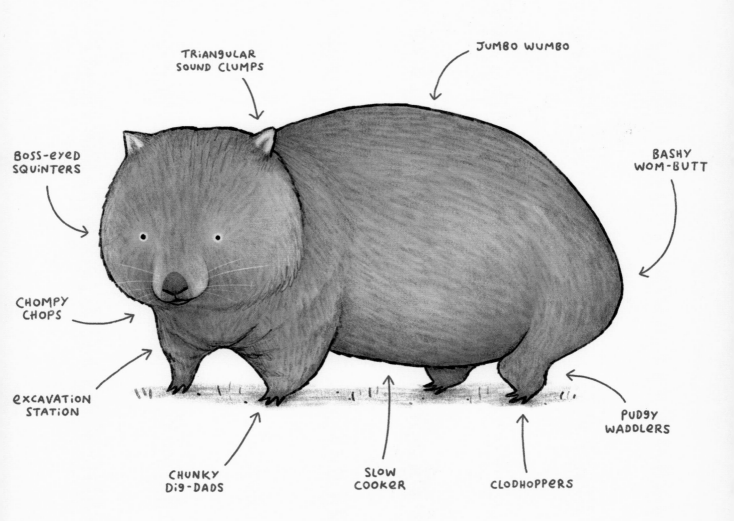

TRIANGULAR
SOUND CLUMPS

JUMBO WUMBO

BOSS-eyeD
SQUINTERS

BASHY
WOM-BUTT

CHOMPY
CHOPS

eXCAVATION
STATION

CHUNKY
DiG-DADS

SLOW
COOKER

CLODHOPPERS

PUDGY
WADDLERS

ANATOMY OF A
SUGAR GLIDER

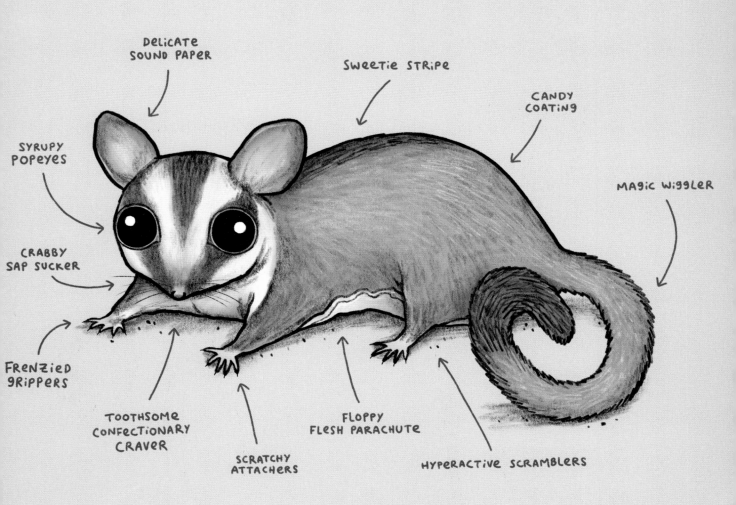

DELICATE SOUND PAPER

SWEETIE STRIPE

CANDY COATING

SYRUPY POPEYES

MAGIC WIGGLER

CRABBY SAP SUCKER

FRENZIED GRIPPERS

TOOTHSOME CONFECTIONARY CRAVER

SCRATCHY ATTACHERS

FLOPPY FLESH PARACHUTE

HYPERACTIVE SCRAMBLERS

ANATOMY OF A CHEETAH

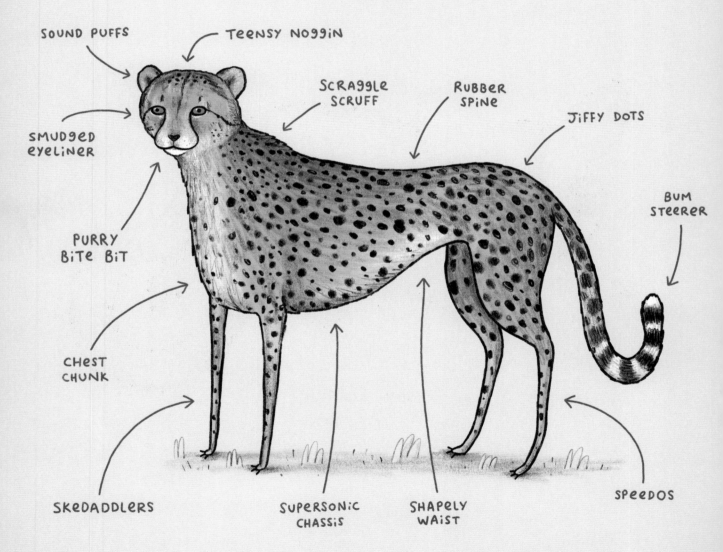

SOUND PUFFS

TEENSY NOGGIN

SCRAGGLE SCRUFF

RUBBER SPINE

JIFFY DOTS

SMUDGED EYELINER

PURRY BITE BIT

CHEST CHUNK

BUM STEERER

SKEDADDLERS

SUPERSONIC CHASSIS

SHAPELY WAIST

SPEEDOS

ANATOMY OF A
SNAIL

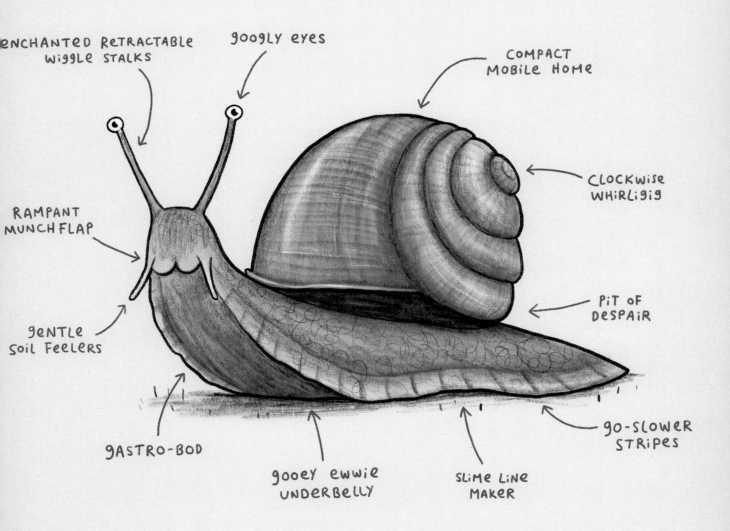

ENCHANTED RETRACTABLE
WIGGLE STALKS

GOOGLY EYES

COMPACT
MOBILE HOME

CLOCKWISE
WHIRLIGIG

RAMPANT
MUNCHFLAP

PIT OF
DESPAIR

GENTLE
SOIL FEELERS

GASTRO-BOD

GOOEY EWWIE
UNDERBELLY

SLIME LINE
MAKER

GO-SLOWER
STRIPES

ANATOMY OF A
gORiLLA

(AKA MiCRO KONg)

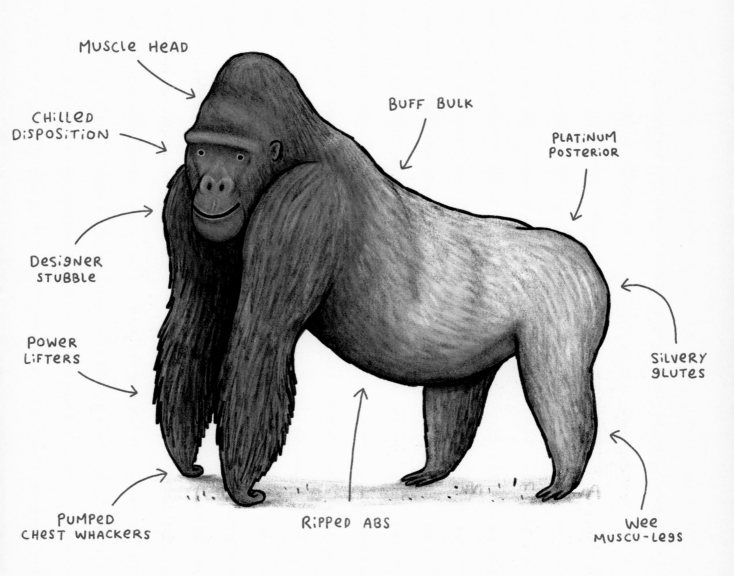

MUSCLE HEAD

CHILLED
DISPOSITION

BUFF BULK

PLATINUM
POSTERIOR

DESIGNER
STUBBLE

POWER
LIFTERS

SILVERY
GLUTES

PUMPED
CHEST WHACKERS

RIPPED ABS

WEE
MUSCU-LEGS

ANATOMY OF AN
ORANGUTAN

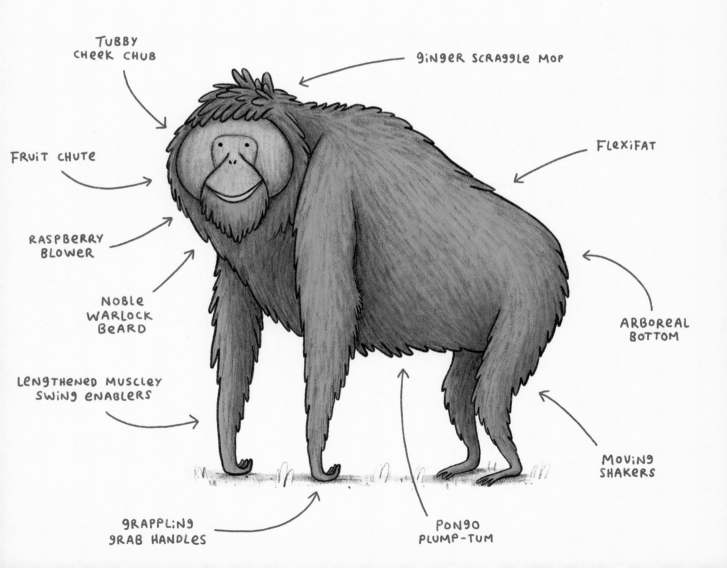

TUBBY
CHEEK CHUB

9in9er scra99le mop

FRUIT CHUTE

FLEXiFAT

RASPBERRY
BLOWER

NOBLE
WARLOCK
BeARD

ARBOREAL
BOTTOM

LENGTHENED MUSCLEY
SWiN9 ENABLERS

MOViN9
SHAKERS

9RAPPLiN9
9RAB HANDLES

PON9O
PLUMP-TUM

ANATOMY OF A
SQUiRReL

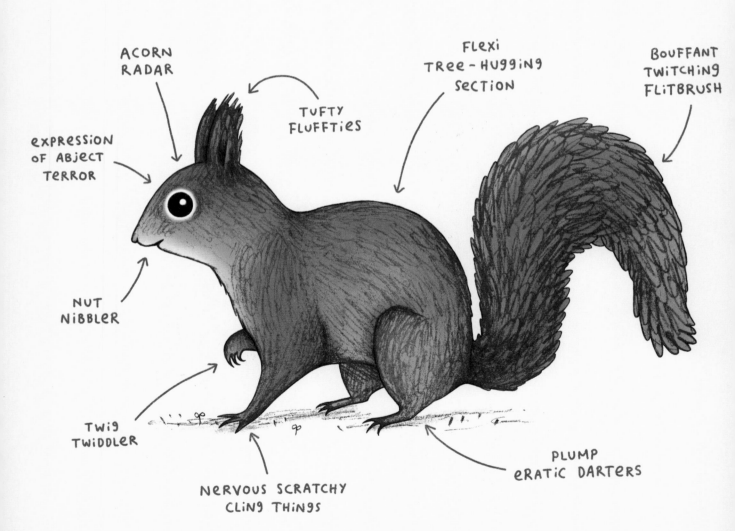

ACORN
RADAR

FLeXi
TRee - HU99iNG
SeCTiON

BOUFFANT
TWiTCHiNG
FLiTBRUSH

TUFTY
FLUFFTieS

eXPReSSiON
OF ABJeCT
TeRROR

NUT
NiBBLeR

TWi9
TWiDDLeR

NeRVOUS SCRATCHY
CLiN9 THiN9S

PLUMP
eRATiC DARTeRS

ANATOMY OF A
SQUiRReL MONKEY

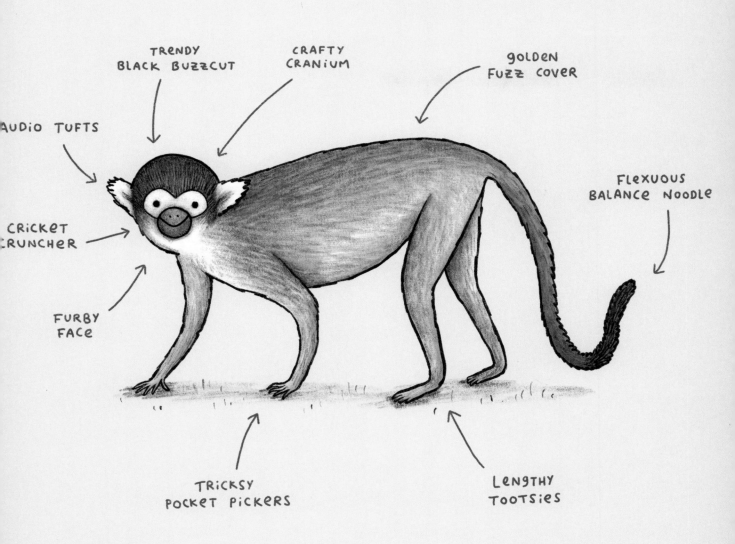

TReNDY
BLACK BUZZCUT

CRAFTY
CRANiUM

gOLDEN
FUZZ COVER

AUDiO TUFTS

FLEXUOUS
BALANCE NOODLE

CRiCKET
CRUNCHER

FURBY
FACE

TRiCKSY
POCKET PiCKERS

LENgTHY
TOOTSiES

ANATOMY OF A
BOA CONSTRICTOR

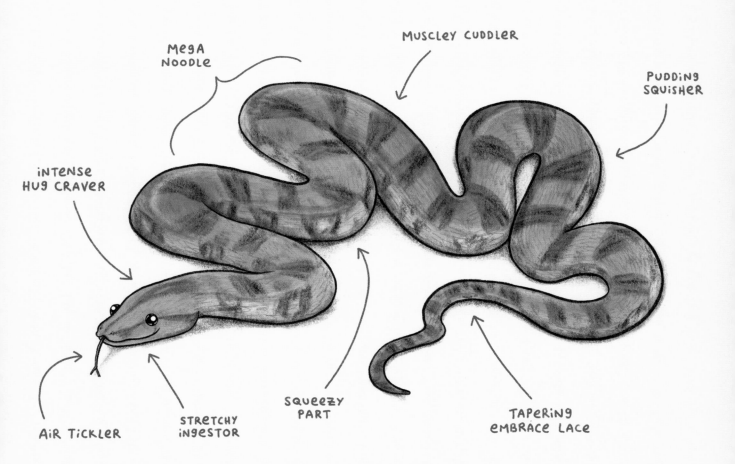

ANATOMY OF A
FLAMINGO

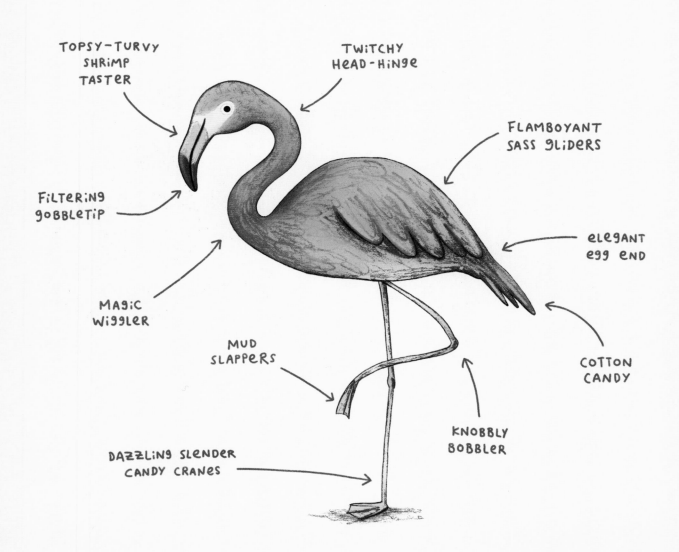

TOPSY-TURVY
SHRIMP
TASTER

TWITCHY
HEAD-HINGE

FLAMBOYANT
SASS GLIDERS

FILTERING
GOBBLETIP

ELEGANT
EGG END

MAGIC
WIGGLER

MUD
SLAPPERS

COTTON
CANDY

KNOBBLY
BOBBLER

DAZZLING SLENDER
CANDY CRANES

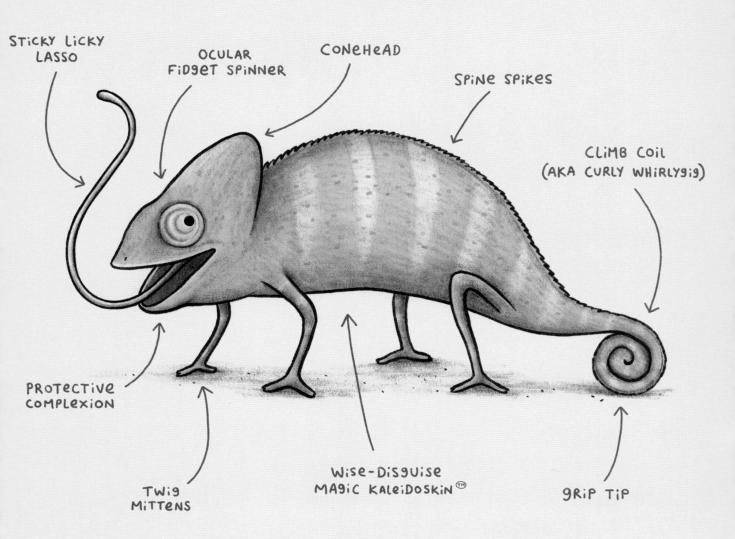

TOUCAN

TOUCAN'T

ANATOMY OF A
MAINE COON

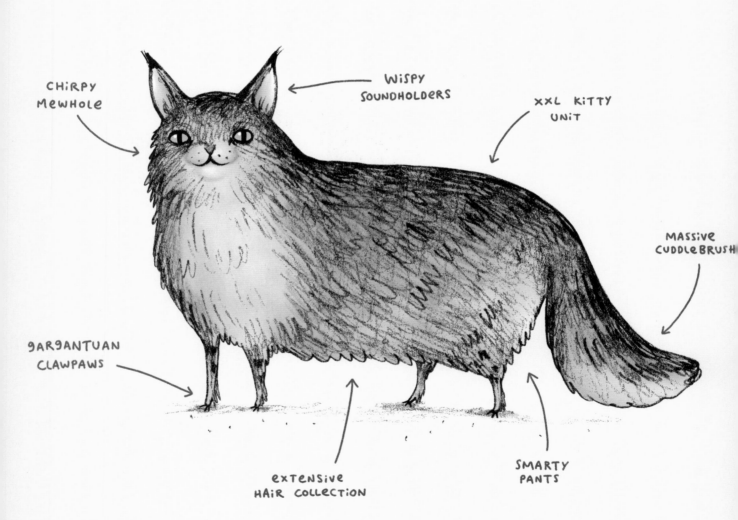

CHIRPY
MEWHOLE

WISPY
SOUNDHOLDERS

XXL KITTY
UNIT

MASSIVE
CUDDLEBRUSH

GARGANTUAN
CLAWPAWS

EXTENSIVE
HAIR COLLECTION

SMARTY
PANTS

ANATOMY OF A
POMERANIAN

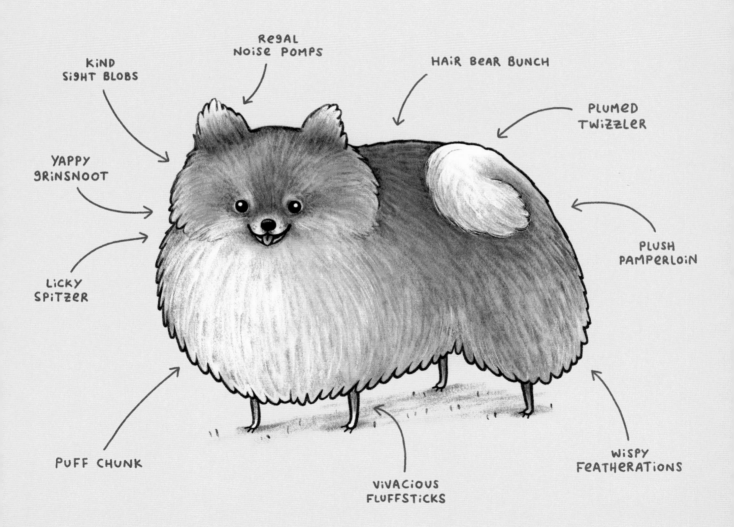

REGAL NOISE POMPS

KIND SIGHT BLOBS

HAIR BEAR BUNCH

PLUMED TWIZZLER

YAPPY GRINSNOOT

LICKY SPITZER

PLUSH PAMPERLOIN

PUFF CHUNK

VIVACIOUS FLUFFSTICKS

WISPY FEATHERATIONS

ANATOMY OF A Moose

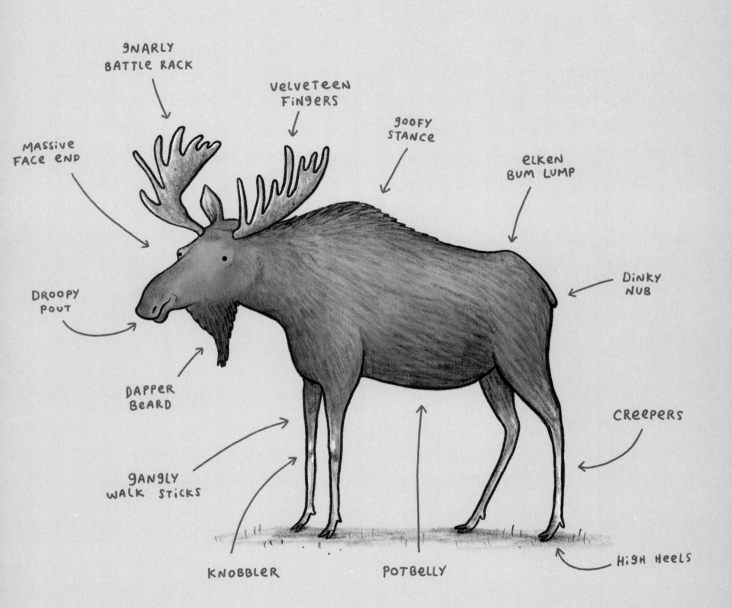

GNARLY
BATTLE RACK

VELVETEEN
FINGERS

GOOFY
STANCE

MASSIVE
FACE END

ELKEN
BUM LUMP

DROOPY
POUT

DINKY
NUB

DAPPER
BEARD

CREEPERS

GANGLY
WALK STICKS

KNOBBLER

POTBELLY

HIGH HEELS

ANATOMY OF A
RACCOON

CUNNING CRANIUM

SHADY GREY
SHAGPILE

BAGGY BOOTY

SNEAKY
BANDITO MASK

RINGED
DUSTBRUSH

NOISY
CUTE-SNOOT

GRIPPY GRABBY
PILFERING TOESIES

GRAY WISPY
FUZZLES

TAPERING
FLUFFENATION

DUST BIN RUSTLERS /
TRASH CAN TOPPLERS

ANATOMY OF A
gRizzly BEAR

POMPOMS

iTCHY
MUSCLE LUMP

SCRUFFLY
COAT

BEADY
PEEPERS

PUMP
STUMP

SENSiTiVE
SNOUT

SALMON
SNAFFLER

DEN
FiLLER

TREEHUGGERS

DEADLY
HONEY SCRAPERS

ANATOMY OF A
9iANT PANDA

FURRY
SOUND TUFTLETS

SLOUCHY STANCE

BAGGY SAGGY
BUMBLING BOOTY

TEENie
ViSiON BEADS

DRAMATIC
eyeLiNER

BAMBOO
BAMBOOZLER

STUBBY
BUTT LUMP

LAZY LeGS

BLACK
HUG BAND

COLOURLESS
PLUSHie FLUFF

ANATOMY OF A
RED PANDA

CAT-BEAR
FIRE FURR

KITTY-LiKE
CURVES

SNeAKY
STeNCH glAND

LiSTeN
WiSPS

SYMBiOTiC SCARF
(AKA SuPeRiOR RiNGed
BuTT CATeRPiLLAR)

SHAPeLY
CHeeKS

KAWAii
CLOWN FACe

BAMBOO
gRASPeRS

FLOPSY
BOD

FLUFFeNATED
STANDY-UP STiLTS

RED PANDAS ARE SORT-OF RELATED TO
GIANT PANDAS, BUT THEY ARE NOT GIANT,
AND ARE MORE RED.

THEY CAN ALSO USE THEIR TAILS
AS SCARVES WHEN IT'S CHILLY...

...WHILE GIANT PANDAS CANNOT.

ANATOMY OF A
SHOeBiLL

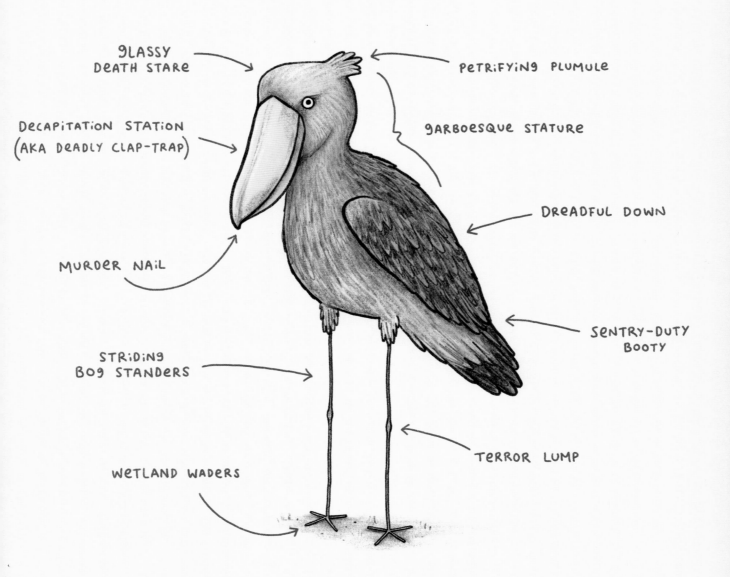

GLASSY DEATH STARE

PETRIFYING PLUMULE

DECAPITATION STATION (AKA DEADLY CLAP-TRAP)

GARBOESQUE STATURE

DREADFUL DOWN

MURDER NAIL

SENTRY-DUTY BOOTY

STRIDING BOG STANDERS

TERROR LUMP

WETLAND WADERS

ANATOMY OF A

DODO

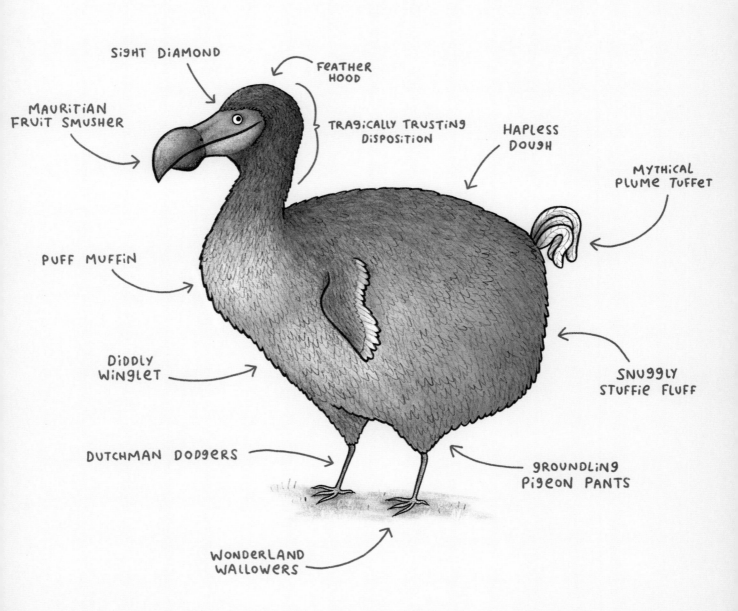

ANATOMY OF A
HUMAN

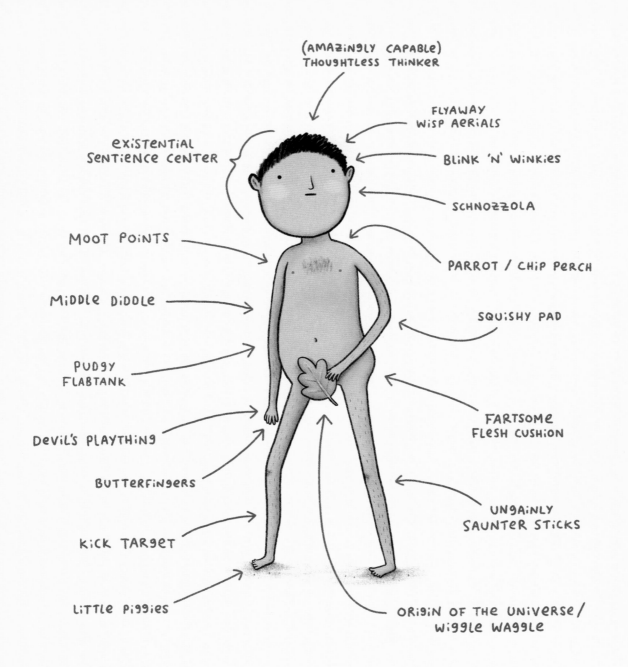

THE END.

ACKNOWLEDGMENTS

For Dad, who started it all with the parson's nose.
Thanks to my wonderful and inspirationally
silly family and friends, who have each helped
immeasurably ~ especially Judy, Keith, Sue,
Matthew, Katie, Syd, Rose, Mel, Louise, Simon,
Tilly, Freya and the many others who have helped
along the way—you know who you are.

Special thanks to Rebecca Hunt and the whole
team of lovelies at Chronicle Books, to Rhea and
Isabella, and to Alex and Mark Gottlieb for
believing in my work.

Finally, thanks to all the cute critters who never
cease to entertain, inspire, and amaze me.

ABOUT THE AUTHOR

Sophie Corrigan is a freelance illustrator who lives above a little candy shop in the UK.

When not drawing and making cute things, she spends her spare time watching nature programs, going to shows, looking for the perfect hot chocolate, and hanging out with her pet axolotls and cockatiels.

First published in the United States of America in 2019 by Chronicle Books LLC.

Library of Congress Cataloging-in-Publication Data available.
ISBN 978-1-4521-7449-5

Manufactured in China.

Cover design by Jenna R. Huerta

Chronicle Books LLC
680 Second Street
San Francisco, CA 94107

www.chroniclebooks.com

10 9 8 7 6 5 4 3 2 1